Something powerful happens when we start to understand and appreciate our own bodies. By inviting us to become **Human Body Detectives**, naturopathic doctor Heather Manley treats us with respect, engaging our curiosity and problem solving skills to consider how our own bodies work -- and why. The more we see about how our bodies build, adjust and repair themselves, the easier it is to make smart choices that we'll be glad we made.

This first case goes right to the core: what we eat is central to great health. Our bodies are built out of food. What we eat can change how we look, how tall we will be, how much we weigh, how strong we are, how we feel, how well we sleep, how well we learn, how often we get sick, and more.

This imaginary journey propels us through the process of digestion -- from food to poop, with some farts in between -- helping us discover for ourselves the beauty of eating a rainbow of great food. Even more than that, I'm excited about the fresh ideas and conclusions these stories will spark in reader after reader. So grab your imagination (the best toy) and have fun!

Alan Greene, MD, FAAP
Founder, DrGreene.com and WhiteOut
Author, *Raising Baby Green & Feeding Baby Green*

Heather Manley, N.D.
www.drheathernd.com

human body detectives®

The Lucky Escape

CASE FILE #1

Dr. Heather Manley

"*ROBBIE!*" yelled Pearl.
"*WHAT DID YOU PUT IN YOUR MOUTH?*"

Pearl ran over to her little brother and pried opened his unwilling mouth. But nothing was there. "Oh, well," Pearl muttered as she turned to her sister, Merrin, who was nestled on the sofa. "Come on Merrin, let's play."

Without glancing up, Merrin replied, "I'm reading an interesting book on the digestive system!"

Real exciting, Pearl thought.

"To digest is to break down food so the body can use it for energy," Merrin explained.

"**WOW**, Merrin, that's sooo interesting!"

Merrin sighed, and continued, "Energy is something you need so you can run fast. Mom always says colorful foods give us lots of running power."

"Oh, I like to run *FAST!* " Pearl said.

"Well, you should eat your  then!"

"Can we please do something else?" Pearl pleaded.

"Pearl, use your imagination. Pretend you're in the book."

Yeah right, thought Pearl. *How could I possibly get into the book?*

With nothing else to do but imagine, Pearl began to see the thing her brother had in his mouth. It was brown and shiny.

She saw it slowly creeping its way to the back of his mouth amongst all this slimy stuff. Pearl shivered. It felt damp and wet. She could see a **dark hole** approaching with something dangling above it.

"OHHH... THIS IS SPOOKY"

Wait a minute. What is going on? Pearl thought.
Am I traveling with that thing? Where am I?

Then she heard the faint echo of her sister saying, "Di...ges..tion..." Something was happening! She felt DIZZY. She tried to scream but nothing came out! She squeezed her eyes shut. Then she heard her sister's frantic cry.

"WE'RE IN A MOUTH!"

Pearl slowly opened her eyes and saw what looked like humongous, white, shiny teeth.

6

Merrin, in complete shock, grabbed her hand and yelled, "Try to stay by the tongue! Look out for that WET stuff."

"What?" Pearl said.

"It's saliva and it softens food so it can be swallowed."

Oh my gosh! Those ARE teeth, Pearl thought. Merrin looked at her sister with panic... They were going to be SWALLOWED!

"HOLD ON, PEARL! WE'RE ABOUT TO GO DOWN THE ESOPHAGUS!"

Pearl noticed that dangly thing and made a frantic leap towards it. She desperately tried to cling to the thing, but it was so slimy she plunged into a pool of saliva.

Merrin, somewhat relaxed, giggled. "Well, you just met the uvula! It makes sure food goes to the stomach!"

The moment their hands touched, they began the dark descent down the esophagus. They clung to each other as they slid down this **moist**, warm tube that connects the mouth to the stomach.

"I feel like Mommy's rubbing my back," Pearl said as she looked at Merrin.

"That's the muscles pushing us. It's called peristalsis."

SPLASH!

They landed inside what looked like a pink bag. It felt wet, slimy, and really gooey.

"Listen! I think I hear a voice," gasped Merrin.

"Girls, I'm putting Robbie down for a nap because he's complaining his tummy hurts," their mom said in a distant, muffled voice.

"That's Mom! She doesn't know where we are," said Pearl.

Then they heard a cry, Robbie's cry, and it was much LOUDER and closer than their mom's voice.

"*I THINK WE'RE IN ROBBIE'S STOMACH!*"
Merrin exclaimed.

"Mom! Mom! Help!!!" they screamed. There was no reply.

Then they heard their mom's soft voice cooing to Robbie, "Come here, sweetie. I'm sorry you have a little tummy ache."

And with that they felt like they were being lifted up and sloshed around.

"Maybe we're supposed to help him. I did see him swallow something earlier. Ohh, we could be body detectives...
Human Body Detectives!" Pearl declared.

She felt something brush her arm and turned to notice a small piece of 🍎 passing by. The girls watched, surprised, as something gooey was squirted on it. It was getting smaller and smaller.

Then something glittery and coppery caught Merrin's attention.

"Hey, maybe that's what Robbie swallowed. But wait... Is it a penny?" Pearl noticed it as well. Realizing what it was, she tried to grab it while singing, "Find a penny, pick it up and then all..."

But just then, a gigantic river of that gooey stuff jetted right next to them.

"Whoa, that was close!" Pearl said, missing the penny.

"Ohh, that stuff must be hydrochloric acid. It makes food smaller, so it can be moved into the small intestine by..."

"AHHHHHH!"

"PERISTALSIS!" Merrin finished. "Hey! Stop bumping me!"

"That wasn't me," Pearl replied.

They turned around and saw at least ten balloon-like things floating around.

"What are those? Is someone blowing bubbles in here?" Pearl asked.

They heard Robbie. "Mama...."

"Robbie, it's okay. Mommy will rub your belly."

Merrin suddenly exclaimed, "Oh my gosh, those aren't balloons, they're gas bubbles and they're going to POP! Robbie's going to fart!"

"*GROSS!*" they both screamed as they were being tossed from one wall of the tiny, pink fingers to the other. Then there was a very loud popping sound.

"Wow, Robbie might be small, but he farts **BIG!**"

Pearl didn't answer.

"Pearl?" Merrin called. She turned and Pearl was not there...

All Merrin could see was a forest of pink fingers, swaying back and forth. "Ohhhh, those pink fingers must be the villi where nutrients are absorbed. We must have moved into the small intestine."

Watching intently, Merrin gasped, " Wow! this is how it works!
The vitamin A in carrots must go through those pink fingers. And then it meets the blood on the other side, which will take the vitamin A to the liver. The liver will receive a message, like a phone call, from the eyes saying that they need more vitamin A so they can see better. So the liver sends the vitamin A up to the eyes."

"*COOL!*"

She felt another bUmP and remembered Pearl. She looked around frantically but only noticed some tiny pieces of 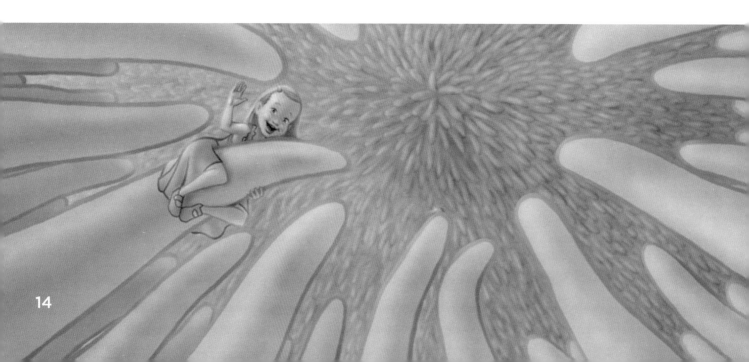 floating by again. Where was she?

Wait. Was that her in the pink trees? "Pearl?"

"Hey, Merrin! Check these out! They're so soft and easy to climb!"

Then, at that moment, Pearl saw the penny and went to grab it. But she missed the penny, fell out of the tree and landed on a minuscule piece of .

"Come on, Pearl. Let's stay together."

Looking down at the , Pearl asked, "Hey, what does Mom say about s?"

"You mean how 🍎s have fiber in them and fiber makes you go poop?" Merrin replied.

They both yelled, "IS ROBBIE GOING TO POOP?"

"Can you feel that? It's per...is.t.., whatever, again!" Pearl said as she spied the penny again. She quickly grabbed it and shoved it in her pocket.

"Peristalsis," Merrin corrected.

The peristalsis wave caught them and splashed them into a new place with lots of WATER.

Where could we be now? Merrin wondered. "Oh wait, I remember. The small intestine is connected to the large intestine. That is where we are, the large intestine!"

"What happens here?" Pearl asked.

"Hmmm... The large intestine moves the WATER into the blood because the body needs water... Oh, no..."

"What?" Pearl questioned.

"Once all the WATER is absorbed into the body, the leftover is waste that the body doesn't need. The body will use peristalsis to push out the waste, or stool."

Pearl questioned, "Stool? Like what we sit on at the breakfast table?"

"No, Pearl. It's poop." Merrin said. "Robbie IS going to POOP!"

"Ewww!" they both screamed as they imagined themselves in Robbie's poopy diaper. Then they heard Robbie. He was tossing and turning and kind of groaning.

Pearl started to panic. "Oh, GROSS! How do we get out of here, and *FAST*?"

Merrin, in a quiet voice, said to Pearl, "I don't know."

They looked at each other in desperation. Then Pearl remembered the penny. Maybe taking it out would help their brother. She fished around in her pocket but she couldn't find it.

"The penny, it's gone!" "We need it to get out! It will make Robbie feel better."

Merrin calmly said, "Check your other pocket."

"Oh, good idea," Pearl said as she dug deep into her other pocket. She immediately saw visions of Merrin and herself sitting on the sofa. She felt safe and comfortable, but very *DIZZY*. The dizzy feeling soon disappeared with the calming sound of her mom's voice.

"MERRIN! PEARL! LUNCHTIME."

Pearl looked at Merrin and opened her clenched hand. And there it was. "It was real! We helped Robbie! He swallowed this penny and we needed to go in and get it!"

Merrin looked at Pearl and the penny quizzically. They silently got up from the sofa and headed to the kitchen table.

Their mom came in from Robbie's room, holding his poopy diaper, which she promptly dropped in the trash.

As their mom washed her hands she said, "Thank goodness Robbie's finally asleep. I think his stomach is feeling much better."

Merrin and Pearl dove into their lunch.

"I'M IMPRESSED. LOOK AT YOU TWO.

EATING YOUR VEGGIES AND ALL!"

"Well, you know, Mom, it's important to eat **COLORFUL** foods," Merrin said.

"It seems your healthy lunch is helping you become smarter. What were you two reading about?"

Pearl placed the penny on the table and sang, "Find a penny, pick it up, and then all day you'll have good luck!"

The girls giggled and they both wondered if there might be more human body detective work to be done someday soon...

human body detectives®

case solved

CASE FILE #1

How good of a detective are you? Can you count all the food images in the book?

broccoli
apple
peas
banana
cucumber
blueberry
sunflower seeds

Let us know how many times you spotted each one at
merrin@drheathernd.com
or pearl@drheathernd.com

More About the Digestive System

The digestive system is the system in the body that is responsible for the breakdown of food, absorption of nutrients from food, and the elimination of the waste and water the body does not need. The digestive system is made up of important organs, parts and chemicals, which all work together to do these things. One might compare the digestive system to a hose that is 25-35 feet long. This would be measuring from the mouth to the end of the large intestine, and taking into consideration that most of the hose is neatly coiled up in a person's abdomen.

The digestive system's main job is to turn foods we eat into tiny particles that the body can absorb and use for energy, maintenance, growth and repair. It also keeps unwanted bacteria or foreign bugs from entering the bloodstream. The stomach and its hydrochloric acid are designed to kill any unwelcome visitors.

i ♥ bolus

The digestive process begins in the mouth with teeth chewing food. **Saliva**, produced by the salivary glands in the mouth, also helps break down food, making it easier to swallow. Once the food is broken down, it is called a bolus. Chewing food is extremely important because it stimulates the brain to tell the stomach that the bolus is on the way. The stomach then gets prepared by producing hydrochloric acid to break the bolus down even more and kill any foreign bugs. The bolus travels to the back of the mouth with the help of a powerful muscle: the tongue! Here, the uvula, or that flap that hangs down at the back of your mouth, helps direct the bolus down the esophagus. The epiglottis is a sort of valve that makes sure that the bolus goes down the esophagus and not the trachea, or windpipe. The esophagus is approximately 10 inches long and the bolus takes about 6 seconds to travel down it and into the stomach. Digestion continues in the stomach and the small intestine with the help of the pancreas, liver and

21

gallbladder. The pancreas produces digestive juices and the liver produces bile, which both aid in further food breakdown. The gallbladder stores bile until it is needed in the stomach. Absorption occurs after the bolus is completely broken down into nutrients. The nutrients will now travel through the lining of the small intestine and into the bloodstream to the liver. The liver stores the nutrients until the body needs them.

Finally, elimination, or pooping, occurs after all the necessary nutrients have been absorbed and only waste is left in the large intestine. Any excess water goes to the kidneys and leaves via the bladder, as urine.

The digestive system is so important to your health. If you take care to eat healthy foods and drink lots of water, and remember to eat slowly and chew your food very well, you are doing your part to help your digestive system do the best job it can, which in turn helps you stay healthy!

The Digestive System

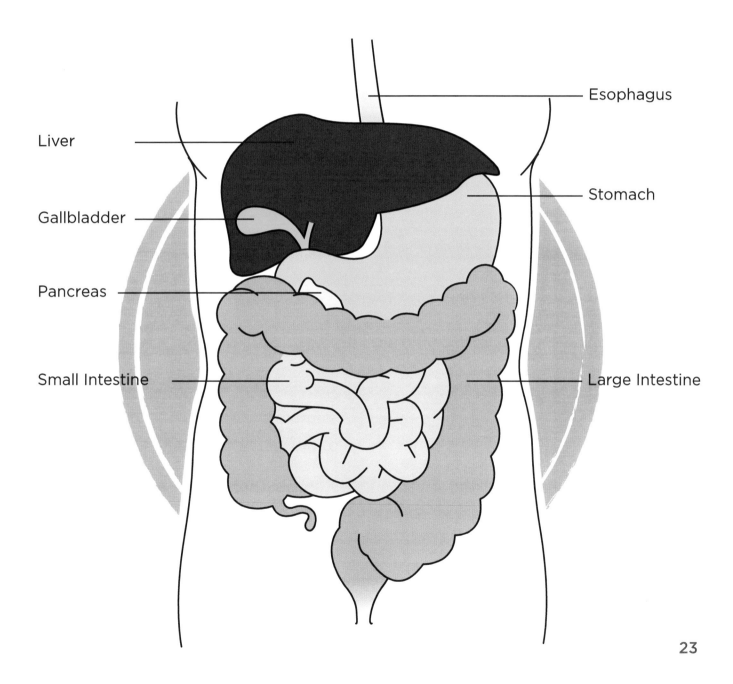

Esophagus

Liver

Gallbladder

Pancreas

Small Intestine

Stomach

Large Intestine

Human Body Detectives Ask You...

Merrin and Pearl have done a lot of reading about the digestive system, not to mention traveling through their little brother's digestive tract. These are some fun facts they learned and want to share with you.

did you know that...

- the stomach has 35 million digestive glands?

- the word "fart" comes from the Old English word, feortan, which means "to break wind?"

- on average, a healthy person farts 16 times a day?

- flatulence (a fart) is a mixture of gases (nitrogen, carbon dioxide, oxygen, methane, and hydrogen sulphide) that are byproducts of the digestion process in humans and animals?

- many animals, including cats, dogs, and horses, fart too? The animal that farts the most is the elephant.

- people fart the most during sleep?

- in an average lifetime, a stomach will digest approximately the weight of a dozen elephants? That's about 50 tons!

- the muscular contractions of your esophagus are so powerful you could drink a glass of water or eat while standing on your head? (Don't try this at home!)

- an adult's intestines uncoiled are at least 25 feet long? Be glad you're not a full-grown horse. A horse's uncoiled intestines are 89 feet long!

- chewing food takes from 5 to 30 seconds and swallowing takes about 10 seconds?

- food can slosh around in the stomach for up to 3 to 4 hours?

- food waste can hang out in the large intestine from 8 hours to 2 days?

- Americans eat about 700 million pounds of peanut butter a year?

- Americans eat over 2 billion pounds of chocolate a year?

Color Your Plate

Not only are naturally colorful foods bright and cheery, they give you all the nutrients that your body needs. When you eat an array of whole foods in all the colors of the rainbow, you can be sure you are getting plenty of vitamins, minerals and phytonutrients (think fight-o-nutrients!), which do all sorts of things in the body to protect you from disease, keep you healthy, help you run that race faster, and think and perform better in school. Unfortunately, not one single fruit or vegetable will give you ALL the nutrients you need so it is best to eat a variety of colorful fruits and vegetables.

So go for it and Color Your Plate! Help out your parents next time you go to the market. Fill your shopping cart with some color, then make that dinner plate look like a rainbow!

red foods

support the immune system
protect your brain
are anti-inflammatory

orange & yellow foods

support your immune system
help your eyes
help your complexion
supply vitamin A

green foods

fight illness
help your heart
help your bones
supply vitamin C

blue & purple foods

support your heart
aid in healthy brain function

proteins

build and repair body tissues

beverages

Water makes up half your body weight and you need water everyday to survive!
Water helps carry nutrients and oxygen throughout the body to properly nourish
it. If water doesn't taste so great try infusing it with slices of lemon or oranges.
(add more color!)

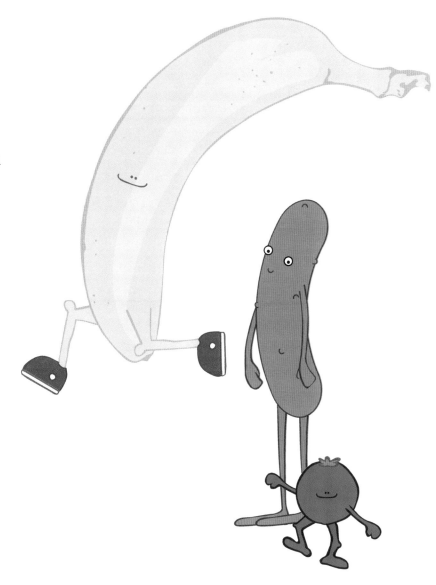

Digest that J●ke

Why was the skeleton afraid to go down the esophagus?
Because he didn't have the GUTS to do it!

What is the strongest and most powerful muscle in the human body?
The MUSCLE SPROUT!

What vegetable would you not want to take on a boat?
A LEEK!

Say this 5 times fast:
Digest that small intestine! Digest that small intestine!
Digest that small intestine! Digest that small intestine!
Digest that small intestine!

Why did the tortilla chips start dancing?
Because they put on the SALSA!

Say this 5 times fast:
Uvula Uvula Uvula Uvula Uvula

What happened to the hamburger that missed too much school?
He had to stay after school to ketchup.

Why did the banana go to the hospital?
He was not PEELING WELL!

How does the man in the moon eat his food?
In satellite dishes!

What do you get when you put three ducks in a box?
A box of QUACKERS.

Why can't you tell secrets in the farmer's garden?
Because the corn has ears and the potatoes have eyes.

What did baby corn say to mommy corn?
Where's POPcorn?

Knock Knock
Who's there?
Bean
Bean Who?
Bean to the bathroom lately?

Glossary

A list of useful digestive words and their meaning.

Bacteria (bak-TEER-ee-uh) There are "good" bacteria our bodies need and there are "bad" bacteria and viruses, which can enter our bodies (like when we catch a cold or a "bug"). Our bodies and our "good" bacteria work hard to get rid of any foreign, unwanted bacteria and viruses.

Bile (BYE-L) Bile is a yellowish liquid that is produced in the liver and stored in the gallbladder. It is needed in the digestive process to help break down foods.

Bladder (BLA-der) The bladder is a hollow, muscular organ that collects urine from your kidney and stores it until you go to the bathroom.

Bolus (BOH-lus) A bolus is food that has been chewed, wet and softened by saliva, and is ready to be swallowed.

Digestive System (dye-JEST-iv SIS-tem) The digestive system is the system in the body that is responsible for the breakdown of food, absorption of nutrients from food, and the elimination of the waste and water the body does not need. The digestive system is made up of important organs, parts and chemicals, which all work together to do these things.

Epiglottis (eh-pih-GLAW-tis) The epiglottis is a flap at the back of the mouth that prevents choking by covering the trachea (windpipe) during swallowing.

Esophagus (eh-SAW-fah-gus) The esophagus is the tunnel passage between the mouth and stomach.

Hydrochloric Acid (hye-droh-KLAWR-ik ASS-id) Hydrochloric acid is produced in the stomach to further break down the bolus. It also kills any unwanted visitors like bacteria and viruses.

Gallbladder (GAWL-blad-er) The gallbladder, located next to the liver, stores the bile that the liver has produced.

Kidney (KID-nee) There are 2 kidneys; one on each side of your body. They have many jobs, one of which is to filter the blood and remove liquid waste, which is then sent to the bladder.

Liver (LIV-ver) The liver is the powerhouse organ of the body. It makes and secretes bile, stores and filters blood, and stores nutrients.

Nutrients (NOO-tree-ents) Nutrients are vitamins and minerals that have been broken down from food during the digestive process. Nutrients help the body function on a daily basis.

Pancreas (PANG-kree-us) The pancreas is located close to the stomach. It secretes digestive juices into the small intestine to aid in the breakdown of food.

Peristalsis (pehr-ih-STAWL-sis) This is a wave-like muscle action that allows for food and waste material to move through the digestive system.

Protein (PROH-teen) Protein is an important part of certain foods (like eggs, meats and nuts) that helps our bodies grow and be strong.

Saliva (sah-LYE-vuh) Saliva is a clear liquid that is secreted by the salivary glands in the mouth. It helps break down food so it is easy to swallow.

Salivary Glands (SA-lih-vehr-ee GLANDS) The salivary glands produce and secrete saliva into the mouth.

Small Intestine (SMAWL in-TEST-in)   The small intestine is the coiled tube between the stomach and the large intestine. This is where digestion and most absorption of nutrients occur.

Stomach (STUM-ahk) The stomach is a bag-like organ located between the esophagus and the small intestine, where food is mixed (almost like a blender) and partially digested.

Stool (STOOL) Stool is unwanted solid waste from the body. It's really poop!

Tongue (TUNG) The tongue is important for tasting foods, licking, swallowing and for us humans, talking!

Uvula (YOOV-yoo-luh) The uvula marks the entrance to the throat. It hangs above the back of the tongue and helps direct food down the esophagus.

Villi (VIHL-lye) These are finger-like projections found in the small intestine that help with the absorption of food.

Dr. Heather is a practicing naturopathic physician who promotes wellness and naturopathic healthcare on her website **drheathernd.com**. She is also the author of the award winning book series, *Human Body Detectives*. Dr. Heather lives on the Big Island of Hawaii with her husband and two daughters, and is currently at work on the next Human Body Detectives adventure.

 tweet with Dr. Heather on Twitter:
twitter.com/drheathernd

Audio versions and apps of all the **Human Body Detectives** books—*Battle with the Bugs, The Lucky Escape* and *A Heart Pumping Adventure*, are available on iTunes.

Visit the **Human Body Detectives** website for free downloads, to view the HBD book trailers, and to watch Human Body Detectives Merrin and Pearl in the kitchen and visiting exciting places!

 visit us on Facebook:
facebook.com/HumanBodyDetectives

LOOK FOR OTHER BOOKS IN THE HUMAN BODY DETECTIVE SERIES:
Battle with the Bugs and *A Heart Pumping Adventure.*

"The pictures are cool! Love the adventure."
Ben, age 12

"It was funny and exciting."
Lucy, age 9

"I liked how the information was so real, but formed into a fun story too. Did you know chewed food is called bolus? I also learned that the thing in the back of your mouth is called your uvula."
Shelby, age 10

"Dr. Manley's stories engaged my kids right away. I like how she is able to tell a fun story yet at the same time teach kids how their bodies work and the importance of making good choices about food and lifestyle to keep their bodies healthy."
Katie, mother

"My kids loved it and wanted to keep on listening. They loved the adventure through the body parts!"
Gregory, father

"The Human Body Detectives puts a fun and interesting spin on the different organ systems in the human body."
Kristie McNealy, MD
www.kristiemcnealy.com

www.humanbodydetectives.com

Made in the USA
Charleston, SC
05 June 2012